TWO THOUSAND MILES TO HAPPY

EARL SHAFFER AND THE FIRST THRU-HIKE OF THE APPALACHIAN TRAIL

By Andrea Shapiro
Illustrated by Rebecca Harnish

muddy boots™

we jump in puddles

Essex, Connecticut

muddy boots™

we jump in puddles

An imprint of Globe Pequot, the trade division of
The Rowman & Littlefield Publishing Group, Inc.
4501 Forbes Blvd., Ste. 200
Lanham, MD 20706
www.rowman.com

Distributed by NATIONAL BOOK NETWORK

British Library Cataloguing in Publication Information available

Library of Congress Cataloging-in-Publication Data available
Names: Shapiro, Andrea, author. | Harnish, Rebecca, illustrator.
Title: Two thousand miles to happy : Earl Shaffer and the first thru hike
of the Appalachian Trail / by Andrea Shapiro ; illustrated by Rebecca Harnish.
Other titles: Earl Shaffer and the first thru hike of the Appalachian Trail

Description: Essex, Connecticut : Muddy Boots, [2022] | Audience: Ages 5-9 | Audience: Grades 2-3
Identifiers: LCCN 2022019779 (print) | LCCN 2022019780 (ebook) | ISBN 9781493068197 (cloth) | ISBN 9781493071029 (epub)
Subjects: LCSH: Shaffer, Earl V. (Earl Victor), 1918---Juvenile literature. | Appalachian Trail--Description and travel--
Juvenile literature. | Hiking--Appalachian Trail--Juvenile literature. | Hikers--Appalachian Trail--Biography--Juvenile literature.
Classification: LCC GV199.42.A68 S527 2022 (print) | LCC GV199.42.A68
(ebook) | DDC 796.510974--dc23/eng/20220519
LC record available at https://lccn.loc.gov/2022019779
LC ebook record available at https://lccn.loc.gov/2022019780

Printed in Mumbai, India, August 2022

THE MOUNTAINS CALLED TO EARL SHAFFER WHEN HE WAS A BOY.

He followed forest trails,
slept beneath starry skies,
and warmed his hands
by a glowing campfire.

IN THOSE MOUNTAINS,
EARL WAS HAPPY.

Earl made a plan
big as those mountains,
wide as the sky,
and glorious as all outdoors.

One day, he'd hike the Appalachian Trail
from Georgia all the way to Maine.

Those distant peaks called when Earl was a man,
lonely and afraid,
while he fought a war on far-off Pacific isles.

When he returned home,
tired and sad,
the Appalachian Trail called once more.

Fourteen states.
Two thousand miles.
Five million steps.
Impossible.

NO ONE HAD DONE IT BEFORE, BUT EARL WOULD TRY.

So, on a blustery April morning in 1948,
Earl stood on a Georgia mountain peak,
beside a weather-beaten sign,
with a pack on his back,
and only the birds for company.

Earl passed a family picnicking by a lake.

"**Where are you headed?**" the man asked.

"**To Maine,**" Earl said.

The woman laughed. "**Glad I've got better sense.**"

MAYBE HE **WAS** CRAZY,

but he hitched up his pack and headed north.

He hiked till daylight turned to twilight.
When storm clouds threatened,
Earl crawled under a fallen tree.
All night he shivered
as a cold rain blew.
But as morning dawned,
he packed his gear
and trudged on.

North Carolina.

Earl struggled up a steep slope,
through face-scraping briars,
over knee-bruising rocks.
Muscles aching and sweat streaming,
he reached the top.
After he rested, Earl walked on.

In Tennessee, by day he wandered past evergreens
to the wind's soft song.

At night, a wild animal's deep-throated cry
sent shivers up his spine.

Three states conquered. Eleven more to go.
He roamed by fields in Virginia
where cattle grazed and farmers plowed.
He sampled fruit from strawberry thickets
and wild apple groves.
He rambled past railroad tracks
and winding roads,
singing a song to lighten his load.

When he heard a rattlesnake's warning buzz,
a cold shiver ran down his spine.

He backed away

and waited

till the snake moved on.

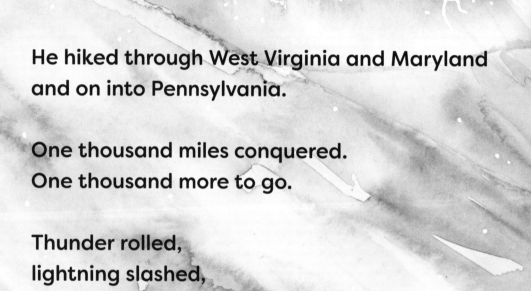

He hiked through West Virginia and Maryland
and on into Pennsylvania.

One thousand miles conquered.
One thousand more to go.

Thunder rolled,
lightning slashed,
and rainwater dripped down his back.

BUT EARL SLOSHED ON.

He walked through New Jersey,
past whitetail deer and lakes and ponds.
He slept in New York under a blanket of stars
to the whip-poor-will's lullaby.

More rain in Connecticut.
Earl still had five hundred miles to go.
His pants were soaked from boot to thigh.
A wire fence blocked the way, so he dropped to his belly
and crawled through the mud.
His murky mood was gray as the sky,
until a man invited him inside.

They shared cookies and coffee
and swapped stories of a far-off war.
Earl's gloom parted like the clouds,
and he was on his way once more.

Warm breezes in Massachusetts
and white birches in Vermont
turned to cold gales
and spruce thickets in New Hampshire.

His boots were cracked.

He carried a smoke-stained pack.

His cooking kit was dented and black.

Earl was tired,

but he still had three hundred miles to go.

One more state. Maine!
One more mountain. Katahdin!
One more mile.

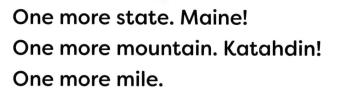

UP! UP! UP!

Giant boulders blocked the way.
A strong wind pushed.
Earl pushed back.

STEP, BY STEP, BY STEP.

Four months, four days, four hours—
through rain, wind, and cold—
on a sunny August afternoon in 1948—
Earl Shaffer stood on a Maine mountaintop
beside another weather-beaten sign.
Patchwork lakes glistened below.

A yodel floated up the mountain
and Earl yodeled back.
He knew the trail would call again,
to walk under snow-white clouds,
to drink from cold mountain streams,
to feel the earth beneath his feet.

Because in those mountains,
Earl found peace.
Earl felt free.

EARL WAS HAPPY!

Earl Shaffer Keeps Hiking

When Earl reached Holmes, New York, he paused to send a simple poem to the Appalachian Trail Conservancy (ATC) announcing his intention to hike the complete trail.

The flowers bloom, the songbirds sing
And though it sun or rain
I walk the mountain tops with Spring
From Georgia north to Maine.

Earl Shaffer was twenty-nine years old when he became the first person to report a thru-hike of the Appalachian Trail (AT). Others had finished all two thousand miles, but no one had notified the ATC of an end-to-end hike completed in one season.

In 1948, Earl followed spring, traveling north, from Georgia to Maine. In 1965, he hiked the AT again, this time following autumn by going south from Maine to Georgia. That made him the first person to report thru-hiking the AT in both directions.

On the fiftieth anniversary of his first hike, he set another record. In 1998, Earl was seventy-nine years old. He walked from Georgia to Maine again, making him the oldest person at that time to thru-hike the AT. With all that hiking, Earl adopted his trail name, "Crazy One."

The trail remained important to Earl throughout his life. He became corresponding secretary of the ATC, advising others in planning thru-hikes. He promoted trail awareness by giving talks, using pictures of his 1948 trek. Earl was active on a local level, too, building shelters and clearing trailways.

Earl's dedication to the trail was surpassed only by his passion for writing poetry, inspired principally by his experiences during World War II and on the AT.

On May 5, 2002, Earl Shaffer died. In 2011 he was inducted into the first class of the Appalachian Trail Hall of Fame, sponsored by the AT Museum Society. Earl's legacy lives on in the steps of every hiker and everyone who loves the natural world and protects the environment as he did.

Further information about Earl Shaffer can be found on the website of the Earl Shaffer Foundation: http://earlshaffer.com/.

Hiking the Appalachian Trail Today

The ATC maintains a list of "2,000-milers" who report hiking the entire trail. Though the organization does not differentiate between thru-hikers and those who complete it in sections over time, clearly the popularity of the trail has grown. From the 1930s to the 1960s, the ATC recorded fewer than sixty 2,000-milers. In the 2010s, that total reached more than ten thousand. These numbers don't include those who use the trail for day hikes or weekend recreation.

Establishing the Appalachian Trail

The Appalachians are a chain of mountains that run along the eastern United States. In the 1930s, volunteers worked to connect existing trails and pioneer new ones to create a continuous two-thousand-mile footpath through fourteen states. It ran through not just federal and state parks, but also along roads and private property. In 1968, with the help of Lady Bird Johnson, President Lyndon B. Johnson's wife, the AT became the first National Scenic Trail. In 1978, President Jimmy Carter signed the Appalachian Trail Bill, which secured protection of the trail.

Preserving the Appalachian Trail

The AT was envisioned as a refuge from urban life, but its proximity to cities has made it vulnerable to overuse. The mission of the ATC is to preserve and manage the trail for generations to come and to serve as the umbrella organization for hiking clubs and other partners such as the National Park Service and the U.S. Forest Service. Thirty-one hiking clubs provide volunteers who maintain shelters, relocate the trail because of overuse or erosion, and monitor the safety of plants and wildlife. Without these dedicated workers, the trail could not have existed for more than ninety years or survive for future hikers.

Further information on the Appalachian Trail can be found on the ATC website: http://www.appalachiantrail.org/.